MW00451085

The
Seasonal Table
Winter

Joanna Quargnali-Linsley

INSPIREBYTES
OMNI MEDIA

The Seasonal Table: Winter

Copyright © 2020 Joanna Quargnali-Linsley
Photography by Alessandro Quargnali-Linsley

All rights reserved. No part of this publication may be reproduced or transmitted in any form or by any means, electronic or mechanical, including photocopying, recording, or any information storage and retrieval system, without express permission in writing from the publisher.

Distributed globally with Expanded Distribution by KDP.

ISBN Paperback: 978-1-953445-96-4
ISBN E-Book: 978-1-953445-97-1
Library of Congress Control Number: 9781953445964

 INSPIREBYTES OMNI MEDIA

Inspirebytes Omni Media LLC
PO Box 988
Wilmette, IL 60091

For more information, please visit www.inspirebytes.com.

Dedication

For all my WINTER friends: those who are the warmth and comfort in cold, dark times… those that understand the value of quiet hibernation space, but also of a raucous candlelight celebration… those that value the waiting while seeds lay dormant, but never forget that the seeds are there under the frozen crust and will soon sprout beautiful things… this book is for you.

THE SEASONAL TABLE

Mark + Kathleen

May all your meals be delicious and filled with love!

♡

Joanna QL

Joanna Quargnali-Linsley

An Invitation

Set an intention to be open about food.

Look at the pictures.

What looks like something you want to eat?
(even if you don't recognize all the ingredients)

What reminds you of a favorite meal in your memories?
What makes you curious?

Contents

Introduction

Why write a cookbook anymore? Everyone seems to have at least a stack of cookbooks, a folder of family recipes, or a ton of printouts from their friends' emails. These days, you only need access to the internet to instantly find a recipe for practically anything. However, a cookbook that inspires you to explore the relationship you have with the ingredients and why you are eating becomes more than a collection of recipes—it's an invitation!

Food isn't just nutritional, it is also medicinal, and its medicine is rooted in tradition. What you crave and eat is a reaction to what you are experiencing. Learning what the signals tell you can change your health and life in the modern world. The seeds were all planted by our ancestors, we just need to recognize them and cultivate them. When we do, it can be beneficial as well as truly delicious.

While this book contains plenty of delicious recipes, it is meant to inspire you with its approach to cooking. It is an approach that focuses on the intention of the meal, while also engaging in conversation with the ingredients and addressing the consumption of more than just nutrients.

When you explore the ingredients you use *in depth,* you learn what they have to offer and whether a specific ingredient resonates with you, personally. By approaching each meal as a love letter, even your most miserable result can taste delicious as the process responds to the love you bring to the making of your food.

As such, this book—this series—serves as a guide to help you explore various ingredients by season allowing them to become your flowery language and descriptive adjectives in the love letter of your meals.

Food Is More Than Timers, Temperatures, and Taste

At a minimum, food gives our bodies the calories we need to survive. At its fullest, it stimulates all of our senses and takes us on journeys that become etched in our minds and memory. Think of your most memorable food moments. Perhaps your memories of favorite meals include the way the sauce stuck to your fingers and had to be licked off. Or maybe you are thinking of the hours spent sitting in anticipation at the table as smells of favorite dishes filled the air. Or it could be visual, as you lovingly remember the sheer abundance of a table stacked with dishes ready to be passed around.

Whatever your food memories may be, just taking a moment to think of them creates a physical reaction in your body. Perhaps you're smiling more, or maybe you're feeling warm nostalgia in your heart. Or perhaps you're lamenting the loss of opportunity to gather together again because life has changed. The beautiful thing about food memories is that they are housed in all five senses and allow us to really connect with both the ingredients and ourselves. They also allow us to connect with others.

My family moved many times while I was growing up, and we traveled often. When I think of my early food influences, I am reminded of all the places we called "home" even if it was only briefly.

I can *smell* the roasted red and green chile and the smoky Pueblo oven bread in New Mexico.
I can *taste* the soft potato dumplings and juicy sausages from a Gasthaus in Vienna, Austria.
I can *hear* the fat melting in smokers and over grills in Texas.
I can *see* the hovering seagulls that begged to share my hoagies on the New Jersey shore.

More than that, I can *feel* the love of my Great Aunt Mary and hear the sizzle as she fried slabs of ham in butter on the griddle at the family farm in Kansas, and I am surrounded by the *laughter* of my Aunt Danita as she made container after container of fresh ravioli, manicotti, and meatballs for me in Chicago.

I believe that food is medicine, but it's more than just medicine for the body; food is medicine for the heart.

* * * * *

The idea of me putting together a cookbook was daunting. I have never cooked by recipe. I take random things from my fridge, freezer, pantry, and yard and make a meal. For years, I have been asked to share my recipes, and I always would find myself laughing in response. Typically, I don't have any idea how much of a specific ingredient I used or how long I cooked a component. I never worried about recreating it, because it was created in the moment at a specific time and place. Food was always about connection, so it seemed odd to me to want to write it down.

My natural inclination to just throw things together had to be put on hold if I wanted to share what I know. I had to learn to measure everything before I put it in the bowl or pot. I had to figure out how to describe the way I cut the vegetables for each dish. And, most importantly, I had to pay attention to timers and temperatures.

I suppose much of my approach to food I learned from my parents. My childhood was a mixed bag of overflowing love and deep trauma, which, not surprisingly, often led to a dysfunctional family dynamic. While there were ups and downs, there was also a lot that I learned simply by being present, and I'm happy to say that my parents are now on my list of best friends and inspirations.

From my dad, I learned the true meaning of persistence and resilience. He embraces challenges and systematically figures out how to get from where he is to where he wants to be. He has amazed me so many times by his nonchalant approach to just "doing the next right thing" and striving to be better. Most notably, he has not let the trials of life stop him, despite the many personal traumas and obstacles he endured.

From my mom, I learned how to creatively complete any project. She can take any item and make it work, whether it's a craft, sewing project, or garden. I once asked her to help me make costumes for a children's pageant I was directing. She traced all the kids on butcher paper, went home to her scrap closet, and came back two days later with handmade costumes that fit everyone. Her flexibility and creativity, as well as her contagious enthusiasm, are awe-inspiring.

My mother is a good cook. Not a great one, but a good one. When my mom *wants* to make something, it is usually spectacular. I have memories of rich tomato sauce with mounds of homemade meatballs, fresh banana bread, calzones hot from the oven stuffed with ham and cheese, and beautifully decorated birthday cakes in the shapes of dolls, bears, and even a carousel. I also have memories of hot dogs thrown in a bun and wrapped in a paper towel to be microwaved for 45 seconds, and bags of frozen fried chicken from a fast food place. (Golden Pride in Albuquerque, New Mexico—I'm looking at you!)

Regardless of how they were prepared, all of these memories bring back a sense of comfort, of nourishment, and of many childhood meals around a dining room table with my two brothers and at least one parent present.

Fast forward to today. When I cook, I want all of the flavors and feelings that come with it. I want the extended meals of summers with our friends in Italy, as we sit outside talking and eating until late in the night. I want the cozy warmth of a hearty stew in a cabin in the mountains after a day of hiking. I want the crispness of a fall evening with a fire pit, a gooey s'more, and a hint of the coming winter biting the air. I want the hope of spring as the first bitter greens and flowers appear to lighten our spirits after months of cold, short days. I want laughter, memories, and nourishment for my heart and soul, not just my stomach.

Reasons for Cooking, Reasons for Eating

Eating—and preparing—your own food, is about so much more than just calories. Every time we eat, there is a reason: hunger, emotion, socializing, routine, or even expectation. Your reason for putting food into your body clearly influences the choice of *what* food to put into your body, but nature itself is a frequently overlooked factor.

The closer I live to nature, the more I understand what foods nature is providing for me. Plants grow in specific climates and at specific times, according to the rules of nature. When I look around and explore the options, I often find that what nature is offering is exactly what my body is craving.

Following a pattern of seasonal eating is the easiest way to eat. Nature has predesigned a menu for us that differs each season and by location. The foods and herbs that are best for our bodies are normally the foods and herbs available to us at any given moment in time at our current location. If we allow it, nature will provide the best guide and choices for us, as she does for the animals and plants that surround us and thrive in our environments.

In the winter, we tuck into our caves with stored harvests of root vegetables and meat. In the summer, we are provided with an abundance of fresh fruits and vegetables that are cooling, nutrient dense, and vibrant with the sun's energy. In the fall, apples fall all around us and allow us to remove the last of our summer heat as we begin to slow down for winter. And, in the spring, nature provides us with dark and bitter greens, like dandelion, to help melt away winter's stored fat.

When people allow nature to guide their choices, they are less likely to eat foods that their bodies are not prepared to process. They are also less likely to be consuming food that contains pesticides, hormones, or other additives to keep it growing and available out of its normal season.

Restaurant chefs must prepare the same food to the same specifications every time they cook. They spend hours and hours perfecting recipes and preparation so that every time a dish is served, it is identical to the last time it was served. We have come to expect this, and if something changes, we complain. Some restaurants create a seasonal menu for this very reason; however, the majority of eating out is rarely aligned with eating seasonally.

Home cooks do not have to be so rigid. As a home cook, I want variety. I want to play. I want to know that I can cook a meal on a Friday night without going to the store because I am two tablespoons short of the butter listed in a recipe. I want to be inspired by what I cook, and more often than not, I find that inspiration in the food itself.

Even when baking, there are few things I make in which I follow the recipe exactly. So much depends on why I am making the dish, who it is for, the weather that day, what I have stocked in my pantry, and how much time and energy I have. And yet, it is not a haphazard approach with chaos and misadventure. It is a journey to discover that I already know what will serve my body, my family, and my friends at my table. I don't overthink what *should* happen. I focus on what *is* happening. In my kitchen, I cook by feel, and then I evaluate afterward what made something taste good, or what was lacking, and how I could do it differently.

Food is also about where you are in your life.

Are you recovering from an illness?
Are you looking for more energy after a good workout?
Are you jet lagged or tired from the stresses of your week?
Are you making multiple meals to lighten the load of an upcoming busy week?
Are you cooking for yourself, your family, or guests?

All of the answers to these questions can influence the choices we make when it comes to eating. The more we listen to our bodies, the more we hear the answer in the food we choose to eat.

While I have shared many recipes from my own kitchen in this book, I invite you to adjust and modify the recipes in the moment, in your space, in your life. What I have captured in these pages reflects a specific mood, moment, or taste in my life. I don't make these dishes in exactly the same way every time. I may add a bit more of one spice, substitute another, or change out the vegetable. Each time I cook, I play.

My hope is that you will use these recipes as an inspiration, and a guide to exploring flavors and combinations. I hope that you will use the spices and herbs that resonate with your culture, background, and needs. My hope is that this food will feed your mind, body, and spirit.

Native Traditions and Wisdom

When I was a teenager, I was taught that when we are in connection with nature, our bodies can heal themselves. My therapist, who was of Native American descent, had introduced me to Ayurveda. Alongside her Native traditions, she had studied Chinese medicine and Ayurveda. She taught me how the five elements of ether, air, fire, water, and earth come together in different combinations to create each of us, and how we each are a mirror of the animal and plant world. My therapist taught me that my evening cup of tea, which I love, could be truly medicinal. She taught me about how spirits show up in animals and plants and guide us if we allow them. It was the beginning of my love for the ancient medicine that surrounds us in every culture, and resides in every family.

In studying Ayurveda, I learned that both Native medicine and traditional European cooking uses spices and herbs that are meant to be tasted. A *dash* of cinnamon is not enough. A *hint* of orange is not enough. A *sprinkle* of saffron just won't cut it. Not only are those not medicinal doses, they are not enough to truly stimulate the senses of sight, smell, and taste. Use a handful, and you will experience what these plants have to offer.

Herbs and spices are the magic in food. They are where all the loveliness and medicine live. Nature teaches that we must stimulate and take care of all the senses. In other words, if you can't really taste it or smell it, you haven't used enough.

Many of the traditional systems focus on the taste—and effects—of food, by category. In Ayurveda, the categories are: sweet, sour, salty, bitter, astringent, and pungent. At home, I strive to incorporate all of these tastes into our daily meals. We frequently have some type of dark greens with dinner, such as: chard, kale, arugula, dandelion, chicory or spinach, to name a few. It's a great way to get some of these flavors in, especially when the salad is made with dried fruit (astringent and sweet), seeds (salty), spinach (pungent), and lemon juice (sour).

I also try to use a variety of spices and herbs in each dish to further bring out these tastes in our meals. While many people in Western (especially American) culture are not often fond of these tastes, I find it exciting to find ways to incorporate them into our meals. Greens are a pretty easy entry point, as are herbs and spices. The key is understanding how to cook bitter and pungent foods in a palatable way, which often involves some type of water, such as boiling, blanching, or soaking. With proper preparation, these taste-filled dishes can become family favorites.

Of course, another point of entry (that doesn't involve cooking) was something I learned in Ayurveda school. One of my teachers had me do an "herb meditation." Without knowing what the plant was, or what part I was being given, I was asked to write two pages about the properties of that plant. I could touch it, tear it apart, smell it, taste it, cook with it, and/or just sit with it. Bottom line? I had to allow myself to *be* with the plant and let it teach me. In doing this exercise,

> I learned that passion flower opens my heart.
> I learned basil helps me think clearly but also keeps me awake long into the night.
> I learned chamomile is like being hugged by every Grandmother I have ever hugged.
> I learned valerian gently holds all my emotional hurt so that I can sort it out.
> I know that mint can warm me up, or make me sweat.
> I know that fresh ginger is wet heat, while dried ginger can suck moisture out of me.
> I know that coriander seed and leaves (cilantro) react wildly different in my body and are not interchangeable.

More important than knowing how to read a label in the store, I learned how to read the plants themselves. Ultimately, however, I learned that every plant had something to offer me, something to teach me, and a medicine to share—if I could allow it to come forth and show me how.

As a result, my cooking tends to follow the Ayurvedic theory while using more American and European herbs and spices. It's this seemingly subtle decision that has made all the difference in how I live, how I work with clients, and how I teach and share what I have learned.

I have seen so many clients, friends, and strangers on the internet desperately looking outwardly for *the* answer. Online, there are posts about what spices, herbs, and fruits will cure every imaginable symptom or disease, from thyroid issues to irritable bowel, to migraines and more. The reality is that no one outside of you has the answer for you.

This Book's Offering

You can research all the various benefits of a specific food for a specific ailment, as there are many books that address this directly by detailing each food's medicinal benefits. I use those books in my private practice as a reference. I read and study them for their detailed information, and I know the various labels of carminative, analgesic, sedative, etc. Even though I have read for countless hours about the properties of plants, I don't remember most of it without looking it up. Looking it up is a place to start the conversation, not a place to end it.

When a client comes to me with a medical diagnosis, my first instinct is to research their condition and find out all that Western and Eastern medicine has to say. I like to look at pathology, prognosis, and treatment options. Inevitably, however, I come back to the human in front me. That human has all the information I need to get things moving. I ask questions, such as: Is there too much stress? Lack of routine? Lack of connection or love? And so much more.

I do not like to tell my clients, friends, or family what "X" is good for. I will rarely explain why the seeds of cumin, coriander, and fennel work best in conjunction with each other. It is always better to let them smell, taste, experience, and know for themselves if that combination serves their best good. All of this is based on a simple truth: Solutions are not "one size fits all" in the plant world. Knowing more about the person and their unique situation allows me to find the best solution for them in a way that will support them on their journey.

This cookbook is similar, it's a path. It's been my path, and hopefully, it becomes yours. It is an invitation to think about food in a new way—the ingredients, the process, and the enjoyment. My hope is that it inspires you to try new things if you are just beginning on this path. If you are more advanced, I hope it serves as a guide to help you tune in more deeply to the medicinal and technical aspects of cooking that nourish our bodies, souls, and minds.

On my own journey, I have had to reinvent myself many times, in many ways. I have devoted my years to studying different things, all of which have culminated in this moment. Whether it was cooking, medicine, gardening, or teaching, I have created a path for myself, and in that process, helped others along their paths.

So, wherever you are on your path, there is opportunity in this book to explore, engage, and reflect on your relationship to different foods, seasons, and why you eat. It is my hope that this book—and the rest of this series—introduces you to a way of living and eating day to day, season to season, year to year.

Winter
BREAKFASTS

Breakfasts

Breakfast is the first moment of the day where we come together as a family; and for me, it's as much about the time spent together as the hot meal that makes it possible, which is why it's so important. I love having this quiet time to check in on any important things happening that day for my daughter at school, and she always asks me what magic my day will hold. Somehow, these conversations don't happen over cereal. But the time it takes to make eggs is enough for her to wander in, sit down, and really be present with me before our day gets going.

We eat a hot breakfast every day during the winter. We often have "standards" like bacon and eggs, or bagels. But we also eat the rice pudding recipe quite often in a ton of different variations. I don't really like oatmeal—I always feel hungry an hour later—but the rice pudding seems to really sustain us throughout the morning. Plus, it smells so good! It's also a great way to get lots of fruit in the cold of winter in a way that is still available (dried). Of course, the flavorful chorizo and potato hash has become a weekend favorite. And eggs in any preparation are always welcome for breakfast in our home.

Chorizo & Potato Hash

½ pound chorizo
½ medium onion, diced (about ½ cup)
1 cup carrots, peeled and diced
2 cups potato, peeled and diced (I use purple and white fingerling potatoes)
1 tablespoon olive oil
½ teaspoon ground cinnamon
salt, to taste (potatoes absorb lots of salt, so don't use salt sparingly)
3–4 cups cold water
4 cups fresh arugula or spinach, washed

Add carrots and potatoes to a saucepan with cold water and cover. Bring to a simmer until knife tender then drain. This should take about 15 minutes.

Heat a non-stick pan over medium heat. Add the chorizo and cinnamon and cook for about 5 minutes. The chorizo has fat that will render out, so there is no need to add oil to the pan first. Break up the meat with a spatula as you cook. Remove the meat from the pan, leaving the fat behind to use for the next step.

Turn the heat down to low-medium. Add the onions and cook until soft, about 5 minutes. Remove the onions and add them to the chorizo.

Add the oil to the pan, then add the drained potatoes and carrots to fry. Add salt to taste. To encourage browning, don't move the carrots and potatoes around too much. Fry for 8–10 minutes.

Remove potatoes and carrots from the pan and toss with the chorizo and onions. Add a bit more oil to the pan and sauté the greens for a minute or two until they are "wilted."

Assemble as you like, with the greens on the bottom or top of the chorizo hash. Optional: add a fried egg or two on top!

Notes on Chorizo & Potato Hash

The potatoes and carrots are boiled first, and then fried. This makes them melty-soft inside, but with some lovely crunchy caramelization of their sugars on the outside. Don't skip the greens! They really make this dish by cutting the heaviness of the fat and brightening the flavors of the rest of the dish.

While this is listed as a breakfast, and we tend to eat it on the weekend as a family, my husband really likes this topped with a fried egg as a "comfort food" dinner on cold Friday nights in the middle of winter.

I created this one weekend when my daughter and husband were camping, and I was getting over a cold. I couldn't figure out what I wanted to eat, so I kept pulling things out of the refrigerator that looked good, and I ended up with this.

You could probably do this with another sausage, but the chorizo has so many spices built in that you would most likely want to up your spices (and maybe change them up) if you use a different kind of sausage.

Eggs en Cocotte

6 eggs
⅓ cup heavy cream
1 teaspoon freshly grated nutmeg (or 1½ teaspoons ground nutmeg)
½ teaspoon ground cardamom
¼ teaspoon ground black pepper
¼ teaspoon kosher salt
2 slices deli ham
¼ cup grated cheese (your choice)
2 tablespoons butter
⅓ cup panko breadcrumbs

Preheat the oven to 375°F.

Coat 4 ramekins with butter. Divide the panko into four and sprinkle into buttered ramekins, coating the sides. Place the ramekins on a baking sheet.

Cut the ham into small chunks and place in the bottom of the ramekins.

Whisk the eggs, cream, nutmeg, cardamom, black pepper, and salt together. Pour the mixture into the ramekins, evenly dividing between the four.

Add the grated cheese to the top of the filled ramekins.

Carefully place the baking sheet in the oven, and bake for 15–18 minutes.

These can be served in the ramekins (careful: they will be hot!) or you can wait a few minutes for them to cool and remove them from the ramekins to serve alone or alongside your favorite toast.

Notes on Eggs en Cocotte

Somewhere between a soufflé and a custard, these baked eggs are filling and delicious. We have used many different kinds of meat but really like them with ham. The spices make them very digestible and cut through any heaviness from the cream and the cheese.

We first tried something like these in a tiny little French café. At the time, I never thought I could make anything like it. It turns out, these are surprisingly easy to make! And if you serve them in the ramekins, you never need to worry about presentation if they happen to stick when they bake.

Breakfast sets the tone for the day. In winter, we do a lot of eggs, bacon, sausage, cooked grains, and other filling things to get us going and keep us going until lunch. These eggs are one of many egg variations that we make on weekdays and weekends.

Breakfast Rice Pudding

2 cups cooked rice or grains
1 cup milk (coconut, almond, or cow's milk)
½ cup or more of extras (dried cranberries, cubed apples, cubed pears, nuts, seeds)
1 teaspoon ground cinnamon
1 teaspoon powdered ginger
1 teaspoon ground cardamom
½ teaspoon freshly ground nutmeg
¼ teaspoon ground black pepper
4 tablespoons maple syrup

Heat the cooked rice, extras, cinnamon, ginger, cardamom, nutmeg, and black pepper in the milk over medium low heat. Let the rice absorb the milk, and allow the extras to soften. Top with drizzled maple syrup and serve.

Notes on Breakfast Rice Pudding

When I make rice, I always make a double batch and put half in the refrigerator in a reusable container. This rice pudding is one of our favorite weekday breakfasts. We use whatever fruit, dried fruit, nuts, and seeds we have. The spices make it easily digestible, and it's warm and cozy feeling. There really isn't a wrong way to make this, so the recipe is not precise. This is also a great way to use up any leftovers from the **Mixed Grains with Dried Fruits** recipe, page 41, in the **Winter Sides** section of this book.

My grandmother loved riced pudding as a dessert, and I remember how good it tasted on a cold night. This is not the same recipe, but has some of the same quality of feeling—like a hug in a bowl. It is a great way to start up a sluggish body on a cold day, and it fills me up for hours. The spices are important to kick start digestion and lymphatic systems in cold weather.

Winter
SOUPS & STEWS

Soups & Stews

Soups are the gateway to being a better cook. They are so forgiving.

My brother called me one Saturday from the grocery store. His wife and son had both just come down with the flu, and he wanted to cook for them. He's newer to cooking, so I stayed on the phone and shopped with him. By using a grocery store rotisserie chicken and adding fresh veggies and ginger, he ended up with a beautiful chicken soup. He said it was the best soup he had ever eaten. He spent all day smelling it and adjusting it to taste how he wanted it to taste, so of course it was amazing!

Don't be scared of soups and stews. It's really hard to get it wrong. Unless you boil off all the liquid, you can always adjust and change it. If the veggies turn to mush, you throw it all in the blender and puree everything into a "creamy" soup. If the flavor is weird, add more herbs, a different liquid, or more veggies. If it's too salty, add water! If it's too thick, add water! If it's too thin, turn up the heat and boil some water off. You get the idea.

Stews are just soups with thicker liquid. The more starch you add—potato, carrot, or flour—the thicker the liquid will become.

A soup made on Sunday can become an entirely different soup on Tuesday when you reheat it and add a cup of chicken stock plus the leftover fried rice from Monday.

Roasted Sweet Potato Soup

2 medium sweet potatoes, peeled and cut in 1-inch cubes
2 large carrots, peeled and cut in 1-inch cubes
4 cups broth (chicken or vegetable work best)
¼ cup olive oil (for tossing sweet potatoes)
2 tablespoons olive oil (for cooking)
1 inch freshly grated ginger (about 2 teaspoons)
1 garlic clove, crushed
¼ teaspoon ground cloves
1 teaspoon freshly grated nutmeg
½ teaspoon powdered ginger
½ teaspoon powdered mild New Mexico red chile (or smoked paprika if you prefer less spice)
salt, to taste
optional: 1–2 cups unsweetened almond milk

Preheat the oven to 425°F.

Toss the sweet potatoes and carrots with olive oil and salt, then roast on a cookie sheet for about 20 minutes, turning them over half way through cooking. They should be knife tender, but do not need to be totally soft. Brown and caramelized spots add lovely flavor.

In a large soup pot, heat the olive oil. Add the grated ginger, garlic, clove, nutmeg, dried ginger, and chile (or other pepper). Cook for 2–3 minutes until you can smell the aroma of all the spices. Add the roasted potatoes and carrots. Stir. Add the broth and some salt. Simmer for 30–45 minutes. Blend the soup—either with an immersion blender or by carefully transferring to a blender. If you are using a blender, do it in small amounts and make sure to vent the top so the soup does not explode. Optional: Add almond milk to thin the soup to your preferred thickness.

Notes on Roasted Sweet Potato Soup

It was a dark and cold Saturday, and my daughter and husband were out for the day, and I wanted soup. I went to the kitchen and started to play and this was the result. It's creamy, and sweet, and yet the clove and chile also make it spicy and warming. Adding the almond milk makes it milder and creamier.

I love roasting root vegetables and adding them to a soup brings that roasted flavor into the soup. One of my friends calls this "Sunshine Soup" because she feels like her insides brighten up and feel warm—like a summer day at the pool—when she eats it.

Roasting the sweet potato and carrot first adds flavor to the soup. This soup pairs well with broiled sausages or grilled cheese.

You could use coconut milk, but as coconut is a cooling ingredient, I don't like how it mixes with the roasted root vegetables and spices.

Regarding the New Mexico red chile powder, I use this in many of my recipes. If you aren't able to find this, you can replace it with cayenne or a blend of black pepper and sweet or smoked paprika, depending on your preference for heat.

Black Bean Soup

1½ cups black beans, drained (canned or pre-cooked from dry; see **Basic Black Beans**, page 39)
2 cups water
1 teaspoon freshly ground cumin
2 teaspoons powdered mild New Mexico red chile (or smoked paprika if you prefer less spice)
1 garlic clove, minced
1 tablespoon olive oil
½ medium onion, diced (about ½ cup)
sour cream (for garnish)

Add all the ingredients (except onions, olive oil, and sour cream) to a saucepan, and simmer for about 30 minutes. The beans should always be just barely covered with water—so keep an eye on the pot, and add water if necessary.

In the meantime, use a sauté pan to heat the oil over low heat and add the onions. Stir occasionally, and let them cook until mostly browned.

Once the beans are tender, but not mushy, mash the beans with a potato masher, whisk, or an immersion blender, as chunky or smooth as you like. Add water to thin to your desired consistency.

Serve the soup garnished with the onions and a dollop of sour cream.

Notes on Black Bean Soup

This is a small recipe I developed to use up the rest of the beans I precook when making **Black Bean Burritos,** page 63. It produces about two 1-cup servings and makes a nice warm addition to lunch. Onions are a common garnish for black bean soup, but I caramelize them in winter to make them easier to digest and to bring some sweetness to this dish.

Beans can be hard to digest. The spices help make the beans easier to digest and make their nutrition more accessible. Sour cream is added fat (and flavor) that complements the protein in the beans and makes the dish a hearty one.

Beef Stew

1 pound stew meat, cubed
½ pound parsnips, peeled and cut in 1-inch cubes
    (about 4, can substitute potato or ½ parsnip + ½ potato)
½ pound carrot, peeled and cut in 1-inch cubes
½ medium onion, roughly chopped (about ½ cup)
2 large garlic cloves, minced
½ teaspoon freshly ground cumin
½ teaspoon freshly ground coriander
½ teaspoon freshly ground fennel seed
½ teaspoon freshly ground mustard seed
¼ teaspoon ground black pepper
1 teaspoon salt (plus more, to taste)
1 teaspoon powdered ginger
¼ cup flour
4 tablespoons butter
4 tablespoons olive oil
¼ cup dried currants (or blueberries)
2½ cups water (enough to almost cover the meat and vegetables)

Preheat the oven to 350ºF.

Mix the flour, cumin, coriander, fennel, mustard seed, pepper, salt, and ginger together in a shallow dish, or brown paper bag. Toss the meat cubes in the flour mixture.

In a dutch oven (or heavy-bottom pan with lid), heat 2 tablespoons oil and 2 tablespoons butter until the butter melts. Brown the prepared meat in small batches, removing it and putting it aside as each batch is browned. Add oil/butter as necessary between batches.

After the last batch of meat, add more oil/butter as well as the parsnip/potato and carrots, and cook to "add color." They do not need to be softened, just a bit caramelized to add flavor to the stew.

With the vegetables still in the pot, add the water and scrape the bits from the sides and bottom of the pot—these are all full of delicious flavor we want in the stew! Add the meat back to the pot, and then add in the currants/blueberries. Tightly cover and place in the oven at 350°F for about 2 hours.

Notes on Beef Stew

If you do not have a dutch oven or other similar pot, do the stove top portion of the cooking in a large sauté pan. Then transfer all of it, including the liquid, to an oven-safe dish with a lid or a tinfoil covering.

I use a cheap metal pie tin to mix the herbs and flour and coat the meat. I have tried a paper bag, and inevitably the meat is wet enough that it soaks the bag and makes a mess. However, I know people that successfully do this, so if you are one of those magicians, do your magic. For the rest of us, I suggest using the pie tin since it is easy to clean up, and doesn't melt when it gets wet.

Parsnips have such a beautiful earthy flavor and are a different starch than potato. This dish is a great place to start exploring how to cook (and eat) parsnips, if you haven't.

This stew is so satisfying. The addition of the dried currants and/or blueberries adds a depth to the flavor that makes it a dish we all want to eat. On a cold, winter's evening, this stew and a biscuit (there's an easy recipe in the **Winter Sides** section) can soothe all the cold bones and aches of a dark night. The spicing is designed to satisfy the need for a good hug, and also help keep energy up and digestion on the right track in a sluggish time of year.

Beef & Barley Soup

2 garlic cloves, minced
1 large carrot, peeled and diced
1 large celery stalk, diced
6 mushrooms, sliced
½ medium onion, diced (about ½ cup)
½ pound ground beef
2 tablespoons butter
3–4 cups stock (chicken, beef, pork, or vegetable)
1 cup dry barley
salt, to taste
pepper, to taste
other spices you might have, such as: thyme, rosemary, oregano
    (I start with ¼ teaspoon of any herb or spice and then smell and taste to see if I need to add more)
squeeze of fresh lemon juice
1 tablespoon grated parmesan

In a soup pot, melt 1 tablespoon of butter, then add the garlic, carrots, celery, and mushrooms, and lightly sauté until the garlic begins to brown. Add stock and stir.

In a large sauté pan, brown the ground beef and onions with the remaining tablespoon of butter. Once browned, you can use some red wine (or other liquid) to scrape up all the bits before adding everything from the pan to the soup pot.

Simmer for about 30 minutes. Add 1 cup dry barley. Simmer for another 15–30 minutes, adding additional water as necessary. (Optional: you can add other spices you have on hand at this point, based on your preference.)

Finish with a sprinkle of lemon juice and grated parmesan.

Notes on Beef and Barley Soup

This recipe was a late addition during the Covid-19 Pandemic.

I was cleaning out my pantry in preparation for a big grocery trip later in the week. I saw a box of "barley soup" and got excited about adding some beef cubes to it and making lunch the next day. When I got ready to make the soup the next day, I realized it was just a box of barley, and not actually a soup. We also did not have any beef cubes, but we had ½ pound of ground beef, so I improvised. It was so good that we ate this once a week until the barley ran out.

If you sauté all the vegetables and brown the meat before adding it to the broth, it will add flavor. However, soups are very forgiving, and you can also just throw everything in the broth and let it cook entirely that way.

Winter
SIDES

Sides

Side dishes are an opportunity for play—and to make bold choices.

In winter, we look for heartier dishes, more fat, and more substantial food to sustain ourselves. Sides are an opportunity to balance flavors and bring out the medicinal aspects of a meal. Having a few bites of something that is strongly flavored can be an adventure. That's why I love bringing in the sweet taste through sides. Adding the sweetness through vegetables can satisfy so much of that desire, that we don't find ourselves overeating or rushing through dinner to get to dessert.

In my kitchen, often the sides are the inspiration for a whole meal. Sides change an otherwise ordinary dinner into an entirely different and magical experience. Adding a bitter green, such as endive, can bring out the flavors of your main dish and make the whole meal seem like a cohesive adventure instead of an expression of: "I eat vegetables because they are good for me."

Buttermilk Drop Biscuits

2 cups flour
2 teaspoons baking powder
½ teaspoon baking soda
1 teaspoon fine sea salt
8 tablespoons unsalted butter, cold
1 cup buttermilk
1–2 tablespoons cow's milk (whole milk is preferred due to fat content for baking)

Preheat the oven to 425°F placing the rack in the middle.

Lightly grease a sheet-pan or cookie sheet, or prepare with parchment paper.

In a medium bowl, combine flour, baking powder, baking soda, and salt. Set aside.

Cut the butter into small chunks and toss with the flour mixture. (I split the butter into quarters lengthwise, and then cut across them every ⅛ inch or so to create small squares of butter). Using your fingers, and with a light touch, rub the butter into the flour mixture until it resembles sand. Stir in the buttermilk and 1 tablespoon of milk. The batter should be very firm but still uniformly wet. If it seems too dry, add the other tablespoon of milk.

Using a 2-inch scoop or large spoon, "drop" dollops of batter onto the baking sheet, leaving about 2 inches between each. You should be able to fit the entire recipe on one sheet.

Bake for 13–16 minutes until the biscuits are lightly golden brown.

Serve warm, with (or without) additional butter.

Notes on Buttermilk Drop Biscuits

I love a good biscuit! These are so easy—and so forgiving—that I love introducing them as an entry point into baking more complicated pastry and biscuits.

Once you get the hang of these, you can add chopped chives, dried herbs that complement the meal, or shredded cheese. These items would be added at the same time as the buttermilk and milk.

We often make a big batch of these to go with soup or stew. The leftovers get toasted and slathered with butter and jam alongside eggs for breakfast, or get stuffed with meat and cheese for lunch the next day.

Cranberries with Ginger

16 ounces fresh whole cranberries
1 cup orange juice
½ cup water
¼ teaspoon salt
2 tablespoons chopped candied ginger (or ½ inch fresh grated ginger root + 1 teaspoon maple syrup)
½ teaspoon ground cardamom
½ teaspoon ground cinnamon
½ teaspoon powdered ginger
½ teaspoon freshly grated nutmeg
2 tablespoons maple syrup

In a medium saucepan, combine all ingredients and cook over medium heat until most to all of the cranberries have popped. Stir often, and adjust water as needed. If you use frozen cranberries, you might need less water.

Let the cranberries cool at least 30 minutes before serving. These are best when they have had some time to sit.

Notes on Cranberries with Ginger

I can usually find candied ginger in the bulk or baking section at my grocery store.

I use whatever orange juice I have. My family really likes pineapple orange juice, and that works well here. Sometimes I add orange, lemon, or lime zest to this dish.

Homemade cranberry sauce is such a controversial topic! Everyone has their favorite or family recipe. I developed this one in Ayurveda school as a balanced way to introduce all tastes in a single dish. It quickly became a favorite recipe in my house and amongst my friends. The tartness and bite of the cranberries goes very well with the richer foods of winter, yet it's still sweet and comforting with the spices and maple syrup such that it isn't too strong even for the picky eaters at my table.

Basic Black Beans

½ pound dry black beans
1½ tablespoons kosher salt (for soaking)
water (enough to cover the beans by 2 inches)
1 tablespoon kosher salt (for cooking)

Add the beans along with 1½ tablespoons of kosher salt to a large bowl and cover with several inches of water. Allow them to soak at least 4 hours, overnight is better.

Drain the beans and transfer to a crockpot or heavy-bottomed pot. Add 1 tablespoon of kosher salt and enough water to cover the beans by 2 inches.

If using a crockpot: cook for 3–3½ hours on high, or 5–6 hours on low, stirring occasionally. If using the stove: bring to a boil for 1 minute and then reduce the heat to a simmer and cook for 1½–2 hours, stirring occasionally.

Beans should be fully tender, but not mushy. Drain before using them in other recipes. Beans take longer or shorter to cook based on the amount of soaking and the age of the bean, so it's a good idea to try them early and adjust the cooking time as needed. This recipe will result in about 3½ cups of beans which is enough to do the burritos and soup in this book.

Notes on Basic Black Beans

Canned beans are incredibly convenient, but can be very hard on digestion. Prepping dry beans is easy and allows you to get rid of most of the non-digestible sugars that tend to cause digestion problems. This is the base recipe to prepare enough beans to make both the **Black Bean Burritos,** page 63, and **Black Bean Soup,** page 19, recipes. All you need is some extra time for soaking and cooking the beans, steps that can be done days in advance (or weeks, if freezing) before you plan on using them.

The spices in the **Black Bean Burritos** and the **Black Bean Soup** recipes help to make the beans more digestible, as well as delicious.

Mixed Grains with Dried Fruit

¼ cup uncooked millet (or other grain, such as amaranth or barley)
½ cup uncooked white rice
1 cup whole milk (see variation below)
1–2 cups other liquid (I use whatever I have: broth, nut milk, stock, etc.)
½ cup chopped dried fruit (apples, cranberries, pears, figs, etc.)
¼ teaspoon salt
½ teaspoon ground cinnamon
½ teaspoon ground cardamom
½ teaspoon powdered ginger
¼ cup unsweetened coconut flakes

Grains and rice should be rinsed to remove the excess and dried starch that they are coated in. Rinse in cool water for 1–2 minutes.

If using a rice cooker, place all the ingredients in the bowl and use the white rice setting.

If cooking on a stove top, add all the ingredients to a small pot and cook according to the white rice package's instructions. About halfway through cooking, add the coconut flakes and dried fruit. You may need to add more liquid than your package suggests, as different grains absorb differently.

Variation: If not using cow's milk, add 1 cup of other liquid plus 1–2 tablespoons of butter or coconut oil as a fat for the dish to cook properly.

Notes on Mixed Grains with Dried Fruit

Any dried fruit works. I like to use dried mango and pineapple. Cranberries are always good in this. Apricots, pears, and apples work well, too. I've even made this recipe with dried figs. More often than not, however, we use a combination of dried fruits.

For a creamier dish, milk or nut milk works well as the liquid, or as half of the liquid. If I'm serving this with chicken, I sometimes do chicken stock as the liquid. Vegetable stock also works well, depending on what you are serving as a main dish. As noted, I often used whatever I have on hand, or whatever flavor I would like to focus on—I just don't use water.

I have made this on the stove top, in the rice cooker, and in a casserole dish in the oven (at 325°F). Each variation produces a slightly different result in terms of texture.

I have also made this recipe as a savory dish. Adding chopped celery, carrot, onion, zucchini, squash, or other vegetables is amazing. For that, I would likely omit the coconut flakes, and maybe add some seeds or nuts instead. The spicing would remain the same for vegetables.

I love this dish because I can make it in big batches and use it for multiple meals during the week.

Endive with Orange Zest

4 endives
zest of ½ small orange (about ¾ teaspoon)
2 tablespoons butter
½ cup chicken or vegetable stock (your preference)
⅛ teaspoon ground allspice
⅛ teaspoon freshly ground nutmeg
salt, to taste

Preheat the oven to 425°F.

Prepare the endive by washing, cutting off the root end, and quartering them lengthwise. Place in rows in a baking dish.

In a bowl, add the stock, spices and salt, and stir to blend. Pour the stock with spices and salt over the endive in a baking dish.

Cut the butter into small cubes. Scatter the butter over the endive. Zest the orange over the endive.

Bake for about 25 minutes, until the endive is soft and slightly browned, and the liquid has reduced to a thick, almost syrup consistency.

Notes on Endive with Orange Zest

Endive is not a popular vegetable in the United States, but it should be. It is most often seen raw in fancy salads. I, however, love it cooked. It is a different flavor, but warms me up on cold winter nights and balances the fats and heaviness of meals in the winter.

Roasted Acorn Squash

2 small acorn squash
¼ cup roasted pumpkin seeds
3 dried figs, diced
¼ teaspoon ground cinnamon
¼ teaspoon ground cardamom
¼ teaspoon powdered ginger
salt, to taste
pepper, to taste
olive oil
2 tablespoons butter

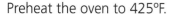

Preheat the oven to 425°F.

Cut the squash in half through the stem and remove seeds. Rub the inside with olive oil, salt, and pepper and place on a cookie sheet or roasting pan, skin side up. Roast for 30–40 minutes until the squash is knife tender throughout. I normally flip them over half way through.

Let the squash cool for a few minutes in order to peel the skin. Once peeled, cut the squash into bite-size cubes. Heat a non-stick sauté pan and add butter. Add the cubed squash to the pan with the cinnamon, cardamom, and ginger. Sauté for 1–2 minutes, then add the pumpkin seeds and figs. Sauté until the figs are soft and the squash is caramelized.

Notes on Roasted Acorn Squash

Squash is a great vessel for a multitude of flavors. Using this preparation, you can substitute any nuts or seeds for the pumpkin seeds. Or you can substitute herbs and spices to your taste. This dish also works well with more heat—like cayenne, red chile, fennel, cumin, and coriander.

Roasted Brussels Sprouts

1 pound Brussels sprouts, cleaned and halved
1 tablespoon lemon juice
zest of ½ lemon (about ½ teaspoon)
2 slices thick-cut bacon, cut into ½-inch pieces
¼ cup dried cranberries
½ teaspoon smoked or sweet paprika (your choice)
2 tablespoons olive oil
½ teaspoon salt (or more, to taste)
pepper, to taste

Preheat the oven to 450°F.

In a large bowl, combine the oil, lemon juice, lemon zest, paprika, salt, and pepper. Add the prepared Brussels sprouts and toss to coat.

Arrange the sprouts on a baking pan, cut side down. Scatter bacon pieces and cranberries over the top of the sprouts.

Roast for about 10 minutes, toss, and roast for an additional 5–10 minutes until the sprouts are well-browned.

Notes on Roasted Brussels Sprouts

Brussels sprouts have a bad reputation. So many of us only ate this as a boiled vegetable on holidays when we were kids. Personally, I always dreaded this as an option until I had them roasted, and now they are a family favorite. The cranberries brighten the dish, and the bacon adds some texture and rounds out the sweetness.

Stewed Carrots with Ginger

2 large carrots (or 3 medium), peeled and cut into coin-sized disks
½ inch grated fresh ginger (about 1½ teaspoons)
1 cup water
¼ cup orange juice
1 tablespoon butter
½ teaspoon salt
¼ teaspoon powdered ginger
¼ teaspoon ground cinnamon
⅛ teaspoon ground clove
⅛ teaspoon ground black pepper
⅓ cup dried cranberries

Heat a pan over medium-high heat and melt the butter. Add the ginger, cinnamon, clove, and black pepper. Stir for about 30 seconds until you can smell the herbs and spices.

Add the carrot slices and stir to coat with the butter/spice mixture. Cook for 2–3 minutes until the carrots have just started to soften.

Add the orange juice and ½ cup of the water and cook over medium heat until the liquid has thickened and about half of the liquid has boiled off. Add the cranberries and the other ½ cup water. Continue cooking until the cranberries and carrots are soft and the remaining liquid has thickened to a syrupy consistency.

Notes on Stewed Carrots

The combination of sweet and savory makes this a great side dish for everything from chicken to pork to beef. It also pairs well with rice, greens, and other side dishes. It may not seem like much, but every time I make this, it is the first dish that is eaten at dinner. No matter how much I make, there are never any leftovers.

Sweet Potatoes with Figs and Goat Cheese

2 medium sweet potatoes (about 1 pound), peeled and cubed
2 ounces dried figs (about 6–8)
2 tablespoons olive oil
½ teaspoon salt
½ teaspoon ground black pepper
1 tablespoon butter
½ teaspoon ground allspice
½ cup orange juice
2 tablespoons goat cheese (about 1.5 ounces)

Preheat the oven to 425°F.

Toss sweet potatoes with olive oil, salt, and pepper. Spread the sweet potatoes out on a baking sheet in an even layer and roast for about 30 minutes, turning them over half way through.

While the potatoes are roasting, remove the stems from the figs and chop them into small chunks (about ⅛ inch cubes).

In a small saucepan, melt the butter and add the allspice, letting it cook for about a minute. Add the orange juice and the figs. Simmer for about 10 minutes until the liquid has reduced and darkened and the figs have plumped up.

Toss the sweet potatoes with the figs and sauce. Top with small chunks of goat cheese.

Notes on Sweet Potatoes with Figs and Goat Cheese

I love sweet potatoes as a base vegetable. I love how you can bring out different parts of the flavor and medicinal properties by how they are cooked. Allspice and sweet potato go very well together. The goat cheese adds a creamy mellow element that helps blend all the bits into a cohesive dish.

Winter
DINNERS

Dinners

Dinner is always at 6pm at my house. And if we have 15 minutes notice, there is a place set for anyone who wants to drop by. The most magical thing is to have a table filled with food and friends. Dinner is so much more than a meal. It is an invitation to sit, connect, and engage with others. In our busy lives, dinner offers us the chance to spend a few minutes on gratitude and the rest on laughter.

These recipes are a collection of things we eat often in winter. Warm, hearty dishes are the centerpiece. Food that takes a bit longer and fills the house with smells of what is to come are the best winter dinners—and there is always something for dessert! We also like to use the leftovers to make great "take to work and school" lunches the next day.

Black Bean Burritos

2 medium sweet potatoes, peeled and diced (about 2 cups)
4 tablespoons olive oil
salt, to taste
2 tablespoons olive oil
2 teaspoons ground cumin
½ teaspoon ground fennel seed
1 teaspoon ground cinnamon
2 teaspoons powdered mild New Mexico red chile (or smoked paprika if you prefer less spice)
1½ medium onions, chopped (about 1½ cups)
2 cups drained black beans, canned or cooked from dry (see **Basic Black Beans** recipe, page 39)
1 cup corn (fresh or frozen kernels)
¼ cup water
1 lime, cut in half
soft tortillas (your choice)
optional: greens, avocado, queso fresco or grated cheddar

Preheat the oven to 425°F.

Toss the sweet potato with olive oil and salt and spread on a baking sheet. Roast in the oven for about 15 minutes.

Meanwhile, in a large pan, heat 2 tablespoons of olive oil over medium heat and add the cumin, fennel, cinnamon, and red chile. Stir the mixture for 15–20 seconds, then add the onions. Cook the onions until translucent and softened (about 3–5 minutes). Add the corn and let it come up to heat (if frozen this might take a few minutes). Add the beans to combine, and lastly add the sweet potato. Be gentle when stirring in the sweet potato so as not to mash them.

Squeeze the juice of one lime over the mixture.

This can be served over rice or in a tortilla as a burrito. We often add some greens like arugula or baby spinach, as well as slices of avocado. Sometimes we go wild and throw some queso fresco or mild cheddar on top, as well.

Notes on Black Bean Burritos

This has become a family favorite "comfort food." There is something about this combination that is both filling and really feels like a decadent treat. I created this recipe in Ayurveda school as a vegan entree, as part of a project on Ayurvedic food for the Western palate.

I never liked beans as a kid, and in fact, I used to get very sick eating them. In Ayurveda school, I learned a lot about what makes them hard to digest, and how to let spices and herbs change those properties so that we can access the amazing nutrition available in beans. I still don't love beans, but I find myself craving this meal as the days get shorter and colder.

Adding greens or avocado can get some extra nutrients and good fat into your meal. My daughter loves avocado, but only on the side. And she likes greens mixed in, but not on the side. I listed them as optional since these are ingredients that families often disagree about. Similarly, cheese can be added at the end based on each person's preference.

Crockpot Spiced Chicken

½ medium onion, diced (about ½ cup)
3 garlic cloves, minced
½ inch grated fresh ginger (about 1½ teaspoons)
1 teaspoon ground allspice
½ teaspoon ground cinnamon
2 tablespoons brown sugar
1 tablespoon lime juice
2 teaspoons salt (or more, to taste)
2 tablespoons olive oil
zest of one small orange (about 1½ teaspoons)
2 boneless skinless chicken breasts

In a crockpot, add all the ingredients. Set the crockpot for 4 hours on low heat, then roughly tear the chicken apart using two forks, and cook an additional hour.

Notes on Crockpot Spiced Chicken

I love winter recipes that cook for hours and make the house smell amazing. I like the spices and the slow build of anticipation. We often make this dish on Sunday and have leftovers for lunches during the week.

This pairs very well with the **Mixed Grains with Dried Fruit,** page 41, or the **Buttermilk Drop Biscuits,** page 33. We have also enjoyed it with roasted potatoes.

We tested this recipe on the stovetop, and it worked well. To do this: cut the chicken into 1 inch cubes and toss with the sugar, allspice, and cinnamon. Heat the oil in a pan over medium heat, add onions, garlic, and sauté until translucent (2–3 min), then add ginger and garlic and cook another 1–2 minutes. Push onion mixture to the sides of the pan and brown the chicken, about 5 minutes. Add broth and orange zest, cover, reduce heat to low, and simmer for 15 minutes or until liquid has mostly evaporated. Add lime and let rest a few minutes in the hot pan before serving.

Turkey Meatballs

1 pound ground turkey
½ teaspoon freshly ground cumin
½ teaspoon freshly ground coriander
½ teaspoon freshly ground fennel seed
½ large onion, minced (about ½ cup)
3 tablespoon olive oil
2 garlic cloves, minced
1 teaspoon kosher salt
⅓ cup panko breadcrumbs (or other unflavored breadcrumb)
¾ cup flour
½ teaspoon powdered mild New Mexico red chile (or smoked paprika if you prefer less spice)
zest of one small orange (about 1½ teaspoons)
1 tablespoon maple syrup
⅔ cup stock (chicken, turkey, or vegetable)

Heat 1 tablespoon oil in a pan over medium-high heat. Add the onion and cook to soften and slightly brown (about 3–5 minutes), trying not to stir them too often. When they are almost done, add the garlic. Cook for an additional 30 seconds and remove from heat.

In a large bowl, mix the ground turkey, cumin, coriander, fennel, onion/garlic, oil and panko. Blend well and roll into balls about 1 inch in diameter.

Roll the meatballs in flour to coat.

Heat 2 tablespoons oil in a pan over low-medium heat. Fry the meatballs in the oil for about 5 minutes. Do not overcrowd the pan. You may need to fry the meatballs in multiple batches depending on the size of your pan. Remove all cooked meatballs from the pan and set aside.

In the same pan, over low-medium heat, add the red chile, orange zest, maple syrup, and chicken stock. Stir gently, scraping the pan as you go to collect the good bits left behind from frying the meat. The sauce should thicken from the flour left in the frying process. Once the sauce has thickened, turn off the heat and return the meatballs to the pan. Gently toss to coat the meatballs in the sauce.

Notes on Turkey Meatballs

Pair these meatballs with your favorite vegetables and side. We have served this with rice, egg noodles, and potatoes. My daughter loves bite sized meatballs, so I experiment with all kinds of different flavors and combinations. These have a sweet and spicy feel that we really enjoy.

In our meatballs, we use different types of ground meat. While these work with beef, we prefer turkey or chicken.

One of the things I love about meatballs is how easy they are to freeze and use on busy nights. I also like that they warm up quickly as a leftover for lunches at work and school.

Fig Stuffed Pork Loin

3 pounds butterflied pork loin (or 2 smaller loins, see note for how to butterfly)
½ medium red onion, chopped (about ½ cup)
6 dried figs, chopped (about ½ cup)
½ cup chopped pecans
3 tablespoons olive oil
½ teaspoon salt
⅛ teaspoon ground clove (+ more for sprinkling)
½ teaspoon freshly grated nutmeg (+ more for sprinkling)
pepper, to taste

Preheat the oven to 400°F.

Trim the pork loin removing any pads of fat as well as the tips so the loin can be rolled smoothly. (Hint: Save the tips for pasta sauce!) Pound the meat thin or make a butterfly cut so it can be filled and rolled. Set aside.

In 1 tablespoon of olive oil, sauté the chopped onions with a pinch of salt until softened, about 3–4 minutes. Remove from heat. Add the nuts, figs, clove, and nutmeg. Stir to combine, coating everything with the spices.

Rub the meat with oil, salt, and pepper on both sides, lay flat. Spread the onion, fig, and nut mixture on top of the meat. Roll the pork loin lengthwise to create a log. Tie evenly using cooking twine every 2–3 inches.

Pre-heat a large skillet or frying pan that can accommodate the roll. Sear the loin for about 2–3 minutes per side until well browned, turning to ensure all of it gets seared. (Add a small amount of oil if the loin sticks to the pan in searing.)

Place the rolled loin in an oven safe baking dish and cook for 30–40 minutes. The pork is done when an internal thermometer reads between 145–160°F. Let rest for 5–10 minutes before slicing.

Notes on Fig Stuffed Pork Loin

Butterflying a pork loin is not as hard as it sounds (though it is very hard to describe in words). There are a lot of videos on the internet that can teach you this skill. The goal is to slice the meat in such a way that the loin opens and lays flat so you can fill it and roll it. You can also just pound it flat or ask your local butcher to prepare the loin for you.

Pork loin can be stuffed with so many things—it's a great canvas for lots of flavors. In the winter, I really like dried figs and nuts. But you can also use soft cheese, apples, cranberries, or apricots, amongst other things. Any spices can be adjusted based on your choice of filling.

I really love making stuffed pork loin for company. It seems so fancy, but it is really pretty easy and forgiving. Plus, the slices always look so enticing and everything smells so good.

The leftovers (if there are any!) freeze well and make great lunches for work or school.

Hint: Costco often sells pork loin in two-packs. Each pack normally has 2 smaller loins that weigh about 1½ pounds each.

Herb Crusted Steak

1 pound steak (your choice)
2 tablespoons olive oil
1 teaspoon maple syrup
½ teaspoon freshly ground coriander
½ teaspoon freshly ground cumin
½ teaspoon salt
¼ teaspoon ground cinnamon
¼ teaspoon freshly ground mustard seed
¼ teaspoon ground black pepper

In a bowl, mix all the spices together and coat the meat, rubbing evenly on both sides. Let the coated meat sit for at least an hour in the refrigerator. (This step can be done in advance, leaving the meat in the refrigerator for up to 24 hours.)

When ready to cook, mix the maple syrup and oil together then rub over the spiced meat.

Preheat a cast iron skillet or other heavy pan over high heat. Cook the meat approximately 3–5 minutes on each side. (Your cooking time will depend on the thickness of your steak and personal preference for doneness.) Let the meat rest for 5–10 minutes before cutting.

Notes on Herb Crusted Steak

My family prefers hanger or flank steak for this recipe. It cooks well, and we slice it into strips. We like to serve our meat medium-rare, so I cut it on a cutting board that collects the juices, and I pour those back over the top.

I really dislike the taste of mustard, but I love using mustard seed in small amounts in winter cooking. It has such a warming and melting quality to it, and it adds a lovely counterpoint to the maple syrup. Mustard seed is an example for me of how you can dislike a plant one way, and love it another. So, if you don't like mustard, start small and try some ground mustard seed. You might find it adds a warmth and depth that is quite lovely.

Leftover Pork Tomato Sauce with Pasta

½ pound pork (Hint: Use the tips from the stuffed pork loin)
½ medium onion, minced
½ yellow, red, or orange bell pepper, diced
2 garlic cloves, minced
salt, to taste
2 tablespoons olive oil
1 teaspoon dried thyme
½ teaspoon ground black pepper
1 whole bay leaf (must be removed before serving)
¼ teaspoon freshly ground mustard seed
½ teaspoon chopped fresh rosemary
½ teaspoon chopped fresh sage
2 cups crushed or blended tomato sauce (see note on page 79)

Chop the pork loin into small cubes, about ¼ inch in size.

In a saucepan over medium-high heat, heat the olive oil until it shimmers. Add the pork and brown it. Try to let it sit for at least a minute before stirring it around. Too much movement will inhibit browning. Once browned, remove the pork from the pan.

Using the same pan, add the onions, lower the heat to medium, and cook until softened, about 2–3 minutes. Add the thyme, pepper, mustard seed, rosemary, and sage. Cook until you can smell the herbs, about 1–2 minutes. Add the tomato sauce and the pork and simmer over low heat for at least 15 minutes. Remove the bay leaf.

Add to your favorite pasta. Or, for a fun idea, use it as a pizza sauce.

Notes on Leftover Pork Tomato Sauce

As with the **Lasagna** recipe, page 81, for tomatoes I like to use jars of "passata di pomodoro" that I can get in the international aisle at the grocery store. It is imported from Italy, and is just tomato. It doesn't need any added sugar or processing. I use it as a base for anything that calls for crushed tomatoes or tomato sauce.

I hate wasting anything, so when I have leftover ends of pork loin from trimming, I cut them into small chunks and put them in a bag in the freezer. This is an easy-to-make tomato sauce that is perfect for any last-minute meal, whether it's with pasta or on a pizza. It's really great in winter with the heartiness of the pork and the heavier spices.

Lasagna

1½ pounds ground meat (sausage, pork, beef, bison)
⅔ pound of grated mozzarella cheese
1–2 boxes of lasagna noodles (your favorite brand)
2 cups tomato sauce (see note on page 83)
½ cup water
olive oil

For sauce

1 small red pepper, diced
1 small onion, diced
3 garlic cloves, minced
1 tablespoon fresh chopped oregano (half of the amount, if dried)
1 tablespoon fresh chopped marjoram (half of the amount, if dried)
1 teaspoon dried rose petals (see the **Winter Herbs & Spices** section for more information)
salt, to taste
pepper, to taste

For cheese layer

¼ cup chopped parsley
1 pound fresh ricotta
1 egg
1 teaspoon salt
¼ cup grated parmesan

In a sauté pan, brown the meat using some olive oil, if needed. Leaving the fat in the pan, remove the meat and set aside.

In the same pan, over medium heat, cook the pepper and onion until softened. Add the oregano, marjoram, and garlic. Cook for 1–2 minutes. Pour in the tomato sauce and add the rose petals. Stir and simmer over low heat, until ready to assemble.

Preheat the oven to 350°F.

In a separate bowl, mix the parsley, ricotta, egg, salt, and parmesan until well blended.

In a large pot, boil water according to your package's directions and add salt. A few noodles at a time, cook the lasagna sheets until just wobbly—there should still almost be a "crunch" if you tried to bend the noodle in half.

Drizzle a few teaspoons of olive oil in a 9 x 13 pan, spread it around to coat the bottom. Add a few tablespoons of sauce, and spread it around as well. Place a layer of noodles to cover the bottom of the pan. You may need to cut some noodles depending on your noodle size. Add sauce to cover the noodles.

Using half of the meat, add a layer on top of the sauce and noodles, then spoon dollops of the cheese mixture on top. Add another layer of noodles in the opposite direction (lengthwise versus horizontal), pressing down to make the lasagna level.

Add more sauce on top of the noodles, then the rest of the meat, followed by the remaining cheese mixture. Add another layer of noodles, again reversing direction. Pour the remaining sauce over the top, making sure to get into all the edges and corners.

Sprinkle the mozzarella evenly over the lasagna. Cover with aluminum foil, and bake for 45 minutes. Remove the aluminum foil to brown the cheese for 10–15 minutes.

Remove the lasagna from the oven and let sit for 10–15 minutes to "set" before you cut it and serve.

Notes on Lasagna

Rose petals brighten the sauce and moderate the acidity. They are my favorite addition to all tomato dishes.

For tomatoes, I like to use jars of "passata di pomodoro" that I can get in the international aisle at the grocery store. It is imported from Italy and is just tomato. It doesn't need any added sugar or processing. I use it as a base for anything that calls for crushed tomatoes or tomato sauce.

This recipe can easily be made with gluten free noodles. Personally, I prefer corn-based noodles to rice noodles. The corn noodles are more easily digestible and more suited to the balance of other ingredients.

There are oven-ready lasagna noodles in the store. I don't recommend them, but they could probably work here.

Lasagna can be prepped ahead, refrigerated, and baked right before you want to eat it, just add a few minutes to the cooking time since it will be cold going into the oven. It also reheats very well for lunches the next day.

Curried Sweet Potato Shepherd's Pie

Sweet Potato Topping

2 medium sweet potatoes, peeled and cubed
4 tablespoons butter
¼ cup milk (or more if you need to thin the potatoes)
½ teaspoon ground cardamom
2 teaspoons maple syrup
salt, to taste

Meat Filling

1 pound ground beef
1 onion, diced (about 1 cup)
1 tablespoon olive oil
1 inch grated fresh ginger root (about 1 tablespoon)
1 teaspoon ground cinnamon
½ teaspoon ground black pepper
1 teaspoon freshly ground coriander
1 teaspoon freshly ground fennel seed
1 teaspoon freshly ground cumin
¼ teaspoon ground clove
salt, to taste
3–4 garlic cloves, minced
½ cup frozen peas
½ cup frozen corn

Garnish

½ teaspoon ground cinnamon
½ teaspoon powdered mild New Mexico red chile (or smoked paprika if you prefer less spice)

Preheat the oven to 350°F.

Prepare the topping:

Peel and cube the sweet potato. Add the sweet potato to a large pan with enough cold water to cover the potatoes and boil until soft. Remove potatoes from water. Mash and blend potatoes with milk, butter, salt, cardamom and maple syrup.

Prepare the filling:

In a skillet pan, heat olive oil and add cinnamon, black pepper, coriander, fennel, cumin and clove. Cook for about 30 seconds, until you can smell the spices and they have absorbed a bit of oil. Add the meat and salt (to taste) and brown.

Remove the meat and set aside. Add a bit more oil to the pan, and sauté the onions for 3–5 minutes. When the onions are about done, add the garlic and ginger and cook for another minute. Add the peas and corn, mixing the onions, garlic, ginger, and vegetables together. Add the meat back to the pan and mix again.

Prepare the pie:

Pour the meat and vegetable mixture into an oven safe pan (I use a 9 inch pie dish). Spread the sweet potato mixture on top of the filling in a thick layer. Sprinkle with cinnamon and mild red chile. Bake at 350° for 20 minutes. For a crusty top, broil for an additional 2–4 minutes.

Notes on Curried Sweet Potato Shepherd's Pie

The red chile can be eliminated entirely, or replaced with a spice of your choice like paprika, cayenne, or black pepper.

The spices in the meat can be replaced with a garam masala blend of your choice. You can often find these in the spice aisle at the grocery store.

This is a great one dish dinner. It can be prepared ahead, refrigerated, and baked right before you want to eat, just add a few minutes to the cooking time since it will be cold going into the oven. It also reheats very well for lunches the next day.

This take on Shepherd's Pie was created one night when I was low on ingredients and substituted sweet potato for potato. I love sweet potatoes with maple syrup and chile. With that modification, I wondered how a curried filling would work. It was an instant winter favorite comfort food! I have made this dish with various types of ground meat and many work, including: beef, bison, lamb, and pork. Personally, I prefer it with ground chicken.

Winter
DESSERTS

Desserts

Desserts should be more about love than calories.

Cookies can be the perfect afternoon "how are you" moment. Cakes can be the "it's all going to be ok" remedy for a hard day. Desserts are love letters to us from past generations. We are inspired by the memories of flavors and smells that come from the kitchens of our mothers, grandmothers, aunts, and cousins. Nourishment comes through all of the senses, including our memories, and therefore, many of us feel comfort around sweets. Desserts are normally considered an indulgence, and people feel guilty when they eat them—but dessert is important for a number of reasons! In Ayurveda, there are lengthy discussions and debates around the sweet taste, but the common understanding is: when it is in balance, we feel more grounded, more loved, and more satiated.

There is an entire industry around "making dessert healthy," but I am not a fan of making something "healthy" just to make it healthy. I don't like to substitute "bad" things for "good" things. I would rather work with the ingredients and find a balance that brings out the best qualities. And then I want to eat that and savor everything it offers from the visual anticipation, to the smell of it baking, to the melty goodness as it hits my tongue. Dessert is no different than any other food when viewed through that filter. Sweets are the thing that most people love, and maybe we just need to tune in better and see how well a few bites of food designed to satiate us can really do the job.

Olive Oil Cake

To follow are two recipes for olive oil cake: **Hazelnut, Chamomile & Cardamom Olive Oil Cake** and **Chocolate Olive Oil Cake**. As such, I thought it would be easier to share my Notes on Olive Oil Cake *before* the recipes.

My Aunt Danita used to make a rosemary olive oil cake, and I really wanted that, but I couldn't find her recipe, and I wasn't feeling the rosemary on a cold Chicago weekend anyway. I wanted chamomile. So, I started by making a list of what I remember was in the recipe and started to play.

I used chamomile that was harvested at the headwaters of the Rio Grande River in Colorado. It has a sweet taste that is also a bit crisp and reminiscent of pine. It's one of my favorite scents. My family and I fell in love with this chamomile cake, and they asked me to make it again right away. I had plans to do so the next weekend, but it snowed and was kind of a horrible weekend. At the last minute I decided I wanted a chocolate cake and modified the liquid and spices to make that happen. The chocolate version was also amazing—and wildly different from the chamomile.

The second time I made the chamomile version, I used chamomile grown in my backyard. It made us all think of summers in our yard and dinners on our deck. One of the things I love about herbs is that they change based on where they grow. Chamomile is one of the herbs that demonstrates this best. I grow two kinds in my yard: one is a standard chamomile sold at garden stores, and the other is from seeds I collected in Italy. My mother also harvests chamomile flowers for me in Colorado. When I work with clients, I pull out all three kinds as a demonstration of the difference. If you smell any one individually, you know it's chamomile. But as you smell them next to each other, you can begin to differentiate the three and guess which one comes from the mountains, which from the plains, and which comes from an Italian villa in the foothills of the Alps.

You don't have to grow your own chamomile for this recipe, you can use a good quality tea. Just rip open a teabag and use the flowers.

Additionally, any nuts could be used for this cake, just make sure they are ground a little. Though, if you like it chunkier, you can just chop them. For this cake, I like it to be almost a powder, but not quite a flour, consistency.

For both cake varieties, it's important to beat the eggs and sugar for long enough. The olive oil is heavy, and the beaten eggs add a lot of air bubbles that keep this cake from collapsing on itself. While the baking powder and lemon will help the rising, the beaten eggs are needed to get enough rise. If you make this with gluten free flour, this is especially important!

This basic recipe is incredibly versatile. You really can play around with it. Just substitute the spices and the addition of the ¼ cup plus 1 tablespoon of flavoring based on what you are trying to make.

Hazelnut, Chamomile & Cardamom Olive Oil Cake

1¼ cup extra virgin olive oil (plus some for preparing the pan)
1 cup sugar (plus about ¼ cup for preparing the pan)
⅓ cup finely ground hazelnuts (plus about ¼ cup for preparing the pan)
2 cups flour
2 teaspoons baking powder
½ teaspoon baking soda
½ teaspoon salt
2 teaspoons vanilla extract
3 large eggs
¼ cup plus 1 tablespoon strong chamomile tea (at room temperature)
1 teaspoon chamomile flowers (stems and pointy bits removed)
½ teaspoon ground cardamom
1 teaspoon lemon juice

Preheat the oven to 350°F. Prepare the pan (9 inch springform, cake pan, or bundt pan) by coating it in olive oil. Then mix ¼ cup sugar and ¼ cup nuts together and dust the pan with the mixture. Whatever doesn't stick can be added to the dry ingredients in the next step.

In a bowl, combine the flour, nuts, baking powder, baking soda, salt, chamomile flowers, and cardamom. Set aside.

In another bowl, beat the eggs and sugar for 3–5 minutes until fluffy and light (see my notes on how important this step is). Continue beating and slowly add the vanilla, olive oil, lemon

juice, and the chamomile tea. Once mixed, slowly add the dry mix until it is all incorporated. Do not over mix.

Pour the mixture into the pan and bake for 45–60 minutes. The cake is done when it feels firm to the touch and a toothpick comes out clean.

Cool, dust with powdered sugar, and serve. This cake is better on the second day after the flavors have a chance to blend and mellow a bit.

Chocolate Olive Oil Cake

1¼ cup extra virgin olive oil (plus some for preparing the pan)
1 cup sugar (plus about ¼ cup for preparing the pan)
⅓ cup finely ground hazelnuts (plus about ¼ cup for preparing the pan)
2 cups flour
2 teaspoons baking powder
½ teaspoon baking soda
½ teaspoon salt
1 teaspoon vanilla
3 large eggs
¼ cup plus 1 tablespoon Kahlua or hot chocolate (at room temperature)
½ teaspoon ground cardamom
½ teaspoon ground cinnamon
½ teaspoon mild New Mexico red chile (or heat of your choice)
⅓ cup baking cocoa
1 teaspoon lemon juice

Preheat the oven to 350°F. Prepare the pan (9 inch springform, cake pan, or bundt pan) by coating it in olive oil. Then mix ¼ cup sugar and ¼ cup nuts together and dust the pan with the mixture. Whatever doesn't stick can be added to the dry ingredients in the next step.

In a bowl, combine the flour, nuts, baking powder, baking soda, salt, cardamom, cinnamon, chile, and cocoa. Set aside.

In another bowl, beat the eggs and sugar for 3–5 minutes until fluffy and light (see my notes on how important this step is). Continue beating and slowly add the vanilla, olive oil, lemon juice, and

Kahlua (or hot chocolate). Once mixed, slowly add the dry mix until it is all incorporated. Do not over mix.

Pour the mixture into the pan and bake for 45–60 minutes. The cake is done when it feels firm to the touch and a toothpick comes out clean.

Cool, dust with powdered sugar, and serve. This cake is better on the second day after the flavors have a chance to blend and mellow a bit.

Chocolate Chip Cookies with an Attitude

1 cup butter (room temperature)
1½ cups brown sugar
1 egg
1 teaspoon vanilla extract
2 cups flour
1 teaspoon baking soda
1 teaspoon ground cinnamon
2 teaspoons powdered ginger
½ teaspoon salt
chocolate chips (8 ounces or more)
optional: ½ cup nuts

Preheat the oven to 350°F.

In a bowl, combine the flour, baking soda, cinnamon, ginger, and salt. Set aside.

Beat the butter and brown sugar until fluffy. Continue beating and add the egg and vanilla.

Slowly add the dry ingredients to the wet mixture to combine using a wooden spoon or spatula. Add the chocolate chips (and optional nuts). Refrigerate for at least 30 minutes.

Use a tablespoon-sized scoop or spoon to roll the dough into small balls and place on greased cookie sheets, approximately 2 inches apart.

Bake for 8–10 minutes until golden brown at the edges.

Notes on Chocolate Chip Cookies with an Attitude

My grandma Ginny was not a great cook. In fact, most of her cooking and baking was terrible in terms of process and technique. But, she put so much love into what she made, everything she made tasted good. Her favorite thing was to bake for days and fill up tins with a few of each kind of goody, before shipping them off to her children and grandchildren. Boxes would randomly arrive with cinnamon rolls and multiple varieties of cookies, brownies, and treats. It was like opening a box of magic every time.

This recipe was one of her guilty pleasures. She once admitted to me that she made extra of these cookies, because she knew she would eat so many before she got around to packing the tins. She even shared that a few times she ate them all and had none left to ship to us! When I was in college, I spent a weekend with her and she asked me to help her bake. The first thing she wanted to make was these cookies, and she gifted me her recipe. Grandma Ginny lived for over 90 years and loved us all so much. When we make these cookies, it's all about her. The heat of the ginger is so warming during a cold winter, and makes these cookies more than "just another chocolate chip cookie."

My daughter bakes with her nanny once a week. One week, they decided to make these and couldn't find the dry ginger. They grated fresh ginger (about 3 teaspoons worth) and used that instead. It worked very well and is an option for a stronger ginger bite.

In this recipe, I have taken Grandma Ginny's original recipe and tweaked the proportions and process to be easier to follow and produce more consistent results. Even though the process may have changed, the love is all still in there.

Coconut Milk Chocolate Fudge

2¾ cups sugar
6 ounces unsweetened chocolate
3 tablespoons butter, plus more for greasing pan
1 cup coconut milk
1 tablespoon maple syrup
¼ teaspoon apple cider vinegar
1 tablespoon vanilla extract
½ cup toasted coconut for top of fudge
optional: 1 tablespoon flower extract like passion flower or rose, or bergamot

Toast the coconut before you start the fudge. Heat a pan over medium heat. Add the shredded coconut and let it sit until you start to smell it. Then move it around as it begins to brown. Remove it from the pan when it begins to turn golden brown, it will burn quickly past that point. Toasting the coconut before you start the fudge allows you to use it when the fudge is ready without introducing heat to the fudge that might wreck it.

Grease an 8 by 8-inch pan with butter.

In a heavy-bottomed saucepan, combine the sugar, chocolate, 1½ tablespoons of the butter, coconut milk, vinegar, and maple syrup. Over medium heat, stir with a wooden spoon until sugar is dissolved and chocolate is melted.

Increase heat and bring to a boil. Once it is boiling, reduce the heat to medium-low, cover, and boil for 3 minutes.

Remove the cover and attach a candy thermometer to the pot. Cook until the thermometer reads 234ºF. Remove from the heat and add the remaining butter. Do not stir! Let the mixture cool until it drops to 130ºF. Add vanilla and stir vigorously with a wooden spoon until well-blended and the shiny texture becomes matte. Pour into the prepared pan and top with toasted coconut. Let sit in a cool, dry area until firm (about an hour). Cut into 1-inch pieces and store in an airtight container for up to a week.

Notes on Coconut Milk Fudge

When I was in Ayurveda school, I did a large project on Ayurvedic cooking for the Western palate. I was looking for desserts that still followed Ayurvedic theory. The recipes I developed at that point included: coconut sugar (less heating than white refined sugar), ghee instead of butter (ghee is refined and offers deep nutrition to our cells), and extract of passion flower, rose, or bergamot. The proportions are the same, but the ingredients are harder to find and more expensive, so I simplified the recipe for more everyday accessibility. Ghee is also much more difficult to balance than butter in this recipe, so I prefer using butter.

Fudge can be challenging to make, but is forgiving in that if you don't get it right, you can remelt it and try again. I find that using coconut milk tends to give a rich and creamy texture and minimizes graininess even if I don't get it perfect.

If you have never made fudge, this might take a few tries, but it's so worth it! If you have made fudge, the process is the same, it's really just tweaked ingredients.

Because of the coconut milk, the toasted coconut is an amazing topping, and my friends all ask for the "toasted coconut fudge" at holidays. I have tried this with almond milk, but the fat content is different, and I haven't quite gotten the smooth creamy dense fudge that I like, so I prefer coconut milk.

Cashew Shortbread

As with the Olive Oil Cakes, I like to find recipes that have a basic core and can be used in a variety of ways. To follow are two recipes for shortbread that are perfect for the winter months: **Chocolate Cashew Shortbread** and **Blueberry Cashew Shortbread**.

These recipes could be made with almost any nut butter. I love the creaminess of cashew butter, but almond butter also works very well and makes the cookies feel more substantial. As there is no need for rising, these recipes will work with a gluten free flour as well. The flour works as a binder only, so gluten free or nut flours will produce a lovely and similar cookie.

Baked goods are a good way to experiment with flavors. Instead of blueberry jam, you could use your own favorite flavor. Rose works well with most fruits, but you could replace that with any edible flower, or leave it out altogether—it just adds a brightness and makes these cookies a bit fancier and more indulgent feeling. Rose also helps cool internal heat and inflammation.

The chocolate variety includes chocolate without making these cookies super sweet. You could remove the heat of the chile if you don't like it. Sometimes, people who are more into savory than sweet appreciate a spicy cookie with only a hint of sugar. The recipe uses melted chocolate to show that it's great done simply. But if you want to do a ganache or something fancier, that is great.

During shelter-in-place, the cookies I made to photograph for this book were made with almond butter since I couldn't find any cashew butter. I also used earl grey fig jam instead of blueberry because that is what I had in my pantry. After doing that, we all wanted to make six more kinds using different combinations, so I'm confident that whatever nut butter and jam you use, these will be delicious.

I love shortbread cookies with coffee or tea. I love making these as gifts, because it just feels very elegant and like it should be harder to make than they actually are. By adding nut butter, they hold together and offer some protein for an afternoon pick me up.

These can be stored in a tin on the counter for about 2 weeks, but they never last that long in my house!

Chocolate Cashew Shortbread

½ cup butter (room temperature)
⅓ cup cashew butter (smooth, not chunky)
1 teaspoon vanilla
1¼ cups flour
¼ cup powdered sugar
½ teaspoon salt
½ teaspoon powdered mild New Mexico red chile (or smoked paprika if you prefer less spice)
½ teaspoon ground cinnamon
2 ounces chocolate chips

Combine flour, powdered sugar, salt, red chile, and cinnamon in a bowl. Set aside.

In a separate bowl, cream the butter and nut butter. Beat in the vanilla. Add the dry ingredients and mix until incorporated. It will be a *very* crumbly dough. Using your hands, form into a 2-inch thick rectangle and refrigerate for at least 30 minutes.

Preheat the oven to 350°F. Remove the dough from the refrigerator and place on wax paper or parchment paper. Roll the dough into a rough 8 to 9 inch square. It should be about ¼ inch thick. Transfer to a clean piece of parchment paper for baking.

Place on a cookie sheet and bake for 12–14 minutes. Let cool for 3–5 minutes, then slice while still warm.

Melt the chocolate chips and drizzle over each cookie.

Blueberry Cashew Shortbread

½ cup butter (room temperature)
⅓ cup cashew butter (smooth, not chunky)
1 teaspoon vanilla
1¼ cups flour
¼ cup powdered sugar
½ teaspoon salt
½ teaspoon powdered ginger
1 teaspoon rose petals (See the **Winter Herbs & Spices** section, page 113, for more information)
2 tablespoon blueberry jam

Combine flour, powdered sugar, salt, ginger, and rose in a bowl. Set aside.

In a separate bowl, cream the butter and nut butter. Beat in the vanilla. Add the dry ingredients and mix until incorporated. It will be a *very* crumbly dough. Using your hands, form into a 2-inch thick rectangle and refrigerate for at least 30 minutes.

Preheat the oven to 350°F. Remove the dough from the refrigerator and place on wax paper or parchment paper. Roll the dough into a rough rectangle about 14 by 7 inches. It will be very thin— less than ¼ inch thick. What's important is that it is twice as long as it is wide, as it needs to fold over onto itself.

Spoon the blueberry jam onto one half of the dough. Fold the other half of the dough over the jam so it is roughly a square. Pat the dough a bit to seal the jam inside. Transfer to a clean piece of parchment paper for baking.

Place on a cookie sheet and bake for 12–14 minutes. Let cool for 3–5 minutes, then slice while still warm.

Winter
NOTES

Winter Herbs & Spices

While I do not believe one size fits all, or that we fully understand all the benefits of these herbs, spices, and plants, to follow is some generally agreed upon information about the ingredients used in this book. These are very simple descriptions and do not cover the extensive known medicinal uses. In all herbal medicine practices, medicinal doses are more concentrated and mixed with companion herbs based on symptoms and treatment plans. All dosages in the book are safe to eat, although I encourage you to notice the effects and adjust based on how you respond. None of this information or the recipes in this book are intended to diagnose or treat any condition.

A note on the use of fresh and dried herbs: In general, to achieve the flavor I want, I begin with ¼ teaspoon of dried/ground or ½ teaspoon of fresh herbs and spices for most of my recipes, and then add more if needed.

There is a debate about the potency and efficacy of fresh versus dried/ground herbs. Medicinally, they may have different properties. *Freshly* dried herbs may have more potency and concentrated flavor when compared to fresh herbs; however, the older the dried herbs are, the less potency and flavor they may have. In medicinal herbal work, older dried herbs are also understood to have less energy or "life force" in them.

In culinary use, as with all other ingredients, I encourage you to find what works for you. I know that dried thyme, marjoram, rosemary, oregano, and parsley have much less flavor than fresh, and I tend to use more in those instances. On the other hand, dried rose has much more flavor than fresh and I tend to only work with dried petals for culinary use. When substituting dried for fresh—or fresh for dried—taste and smell will always be your best guide to determine the amounts you like in your food. Food as medicine speaks to the balanced whole, and not any single ingredient or dish. As such, it's important for you to experiment and find your own balance in making these, or any other, recipes.

Allspice is a berry that comes from an aromatic evergreen tree. You can grind the berries yourself or purchase them powdered. Allspice is most commonly found in fall desserts in the Western diet. It is used in chutneys, jerk blends, and condiments in the Caribbean. It has similar properties to clove with a milder taste, in that it aids in sluggish digestion.

Black Pepper comes from a perennial woody plant that produces clusters of fruit "berries" that are picked at various stages of ripeness and dried. Black peppercorns are sold whole, typically in grinders, as well as in bulk at the grocery store. Pre-ground pepper is found in the spice section. It is used for digestion, as well as respiratory and circulatory conditions. Black pepper tastes sharp—like a small little burst of something—then mellows out.

Cardamom is an aromatic seed pod. The seed pod is green and the seeds are reddish brown. It is most often sold dried and powdered. Its seeds (found in the pod) help with digestion and reduce mucus. It has a sweet taste and often makes people think of limes.

Chamomile Flowers are aromatic with a slightly bitter taste. There are many varieties and relatives worldwide. In the Southwest and Western US, you can often find wild pineapple weed which looks like chamomile (minus the white petals), shares medicinal properties, and is often made into a tea. It has a calming effect on the nervous system and on digestion. Chamomile can taste different depending on where it grew. It can range from almost minty, to a citrus taste, to an earthy bitter. I recommend you try to find a local source or two to discover what you like best.

Cinnamon is the bark of a tree. It protects and strengthens the intestines. It can be found powdered in the spice section or in tight, dried rolls that look like straws. I tend to use the powdered unless I want more of an infusion where I will use the bark and then remove it from the dish before serving. Cinnamon has a light heat and is a taste most people recognize from baked goods, but may find they enjoy in savory dishes as well.

Cloves are the dried flower buds of the clove tree. They help with sluggish digestion and are aromatic. While it's possible to grind whole cloves, it is much easier to buy these powdered. Clove has a strong, distinct taste. When used in small amounts, that strong taste blends well with other aromatics.

Coriander Seed comes from the Cilantro plant. In Europe, the leaves are also called coriander, but in North America, we tend to refer to leaves as cilantro and seeds as coriander. These seeds are round in contrast to fennel and cumin. They have a hard shell and taste like dried, mild cilantro. I grind these myself, but you can also find them powdered in the spice section of the grocery store. Fennel, cumin and coriander seeds are often used as a combination in Ayurvedic cooking and medicine.

Cumin Seeds are from a small shrubby annual. Its name in Sanskrit means "promoting digestion." It is a small thin seed. I like to grind this one myself, but you can also find it powdered. It has been a popular herb since the Ancient Egyptians cultivated it. Cumin seeds can help with nutrient absorption when used in cooking. They are mild and have a gentle bite to the taste. Fennel, cumin, and coriander seeds are often used as a combination in Ayurvedic cooking and medicine.

Fennel Seed are the seeds found when a fennel bulb flowers. The fennel plant is edible from root to fronds to stalks to seeds. The seeds are aromatic and famed for their uses in aiding digestion. Fennel seed is semi-floral and earthy to taste. Fennel, cumin, and coriander seeds are often used as a combination in Ayurvedic cooking and medicine.

Garlic is a bulb that is harvested and then partially dried. If you find garlic to be bitter, remove the center from the clove (it is often tinged yellow or green) and the bitter taste will go away. I like to crush garlic bulbs myself, but I know plenty of people who buy jars of minced garlic and are happy using it. Garlic definitely has a bite and leaves a smell on fingers and breath. Hopefully you are surrounded by people who like the smell.

Ginger is a perennial plant that grows up to two feet tall and blooms with white or yellow flowers. The root has a golden brown skin and a yellow fibrous flesh. The **fresh** root is available in the produce section of many grocery stores. After peeling, you can crush, chop, grate, or juice the flesh. The **dried** root is peeled and then powdered. Ginger is called the "universal medicine" in Ayurveda and often used for digestion, lungs, and circulation. It is heating, particularly in the dried form so caution is advised for some conditions when taken in larger, medicinal doses. Ginger has a bite to the taste that is immediately warming in both forms.

Maple Syrup is made by reducing the liquid (sap) that flows through maple trees in the early spring to carry nutrients. It is considered to be a "pre-digested" sugar and therefore more suitable than white sugar for metabolizing. It also does not have a "hot" effect like white sugar and is therefore considered to be preferable to white sugar. It is moistening and can soothe winter dryness and aching joints. Maple syrup is luxuriously sweet and gooey.

Mustard Seed comes from a flowering plant. Many people also eat the greens. The seed is dried and is good for clearing sluggishness from the digestion and the lungs. The seeds are often available in bulk sections and can be ground in a spice grinder or with a mortar and pestle. I find mustard seed to have a warm and earthy taste.

Nutmeg is the fruit seed of a dark-leafed evergreen. It resembles a fruit "pit," and can be grated or found in a powdered form. I prefer freshly grated. Nutmeg helps with digestion and calming the nervous system. Nutmeg is a subtle flavor that most people do not recognize right away but find soothing as they begin to identify with it.

Red Chile and other "hot red pepper" like Cayenne are truly a preference and extremely regional. I refer to the New Mexico red chile powder in several recipes in the book. If this is unavailable to you, you can substitute with either cayenne, or a blend of black pepper and smoked paprika. While these peppers are all loosely related, they will have different medicinal impacts. In general, they are all heating, can induce sweating, increase blood flow to skin and the extremities, and aid in digestion. In small amounts, or with mild chiles, the taste is warming and vibrant.

Rose Petals are dried and crumbled when used in food. Please make sure you have organic petals if you wish to try using them. They have an affinity for the heart, and are used for the vascular system and as a mild nervine sedative. The smell and the taste are said to "lift the spirits." I buy these in bulk from a local farm, but they can be found in natural food stores and online. They taste like they smell. When used in sweets, they should be used sparingly as they can quickly overpower other flavors. In combination with acidic foods like tomato, they bring out a fruity, floral taste in the dish,

Salt is either mined or distilled from sea water. One of the most important things about salt, is that it brings out and amplifies flavor, and "sets" the flavors once combined. Salting during the cooking process is more beneficial than adding salt at the end. While there are many disagreements on the benefit of salt, I list it here because of how it enhances flavors when used correctly. Everyone recognizes the taste of salt, but the goal should be to not taste it. If the use of salt is well balanced, you will taste everything else better, without tasting the salt.

About the Author

Joanna Quargnali-Linsley combines her training and experience in both Eastern and Western traditions to create meaningful, flavor-centric meals that both inspire and create a sense of connectedness—to each other, to nature, and to our own bodies.

From an early age, Joanna has been passionate about advocating for others. Her varied career coalesced and led to her becoming who she always was: a "Pathfinder"—one who helps others move through uncertain challenges using skills she has acquired through her own diverse experiences. After having to navigate the medical system for multiple family members with rare conditions, Joanna returned to school to become a Certified Ayurvedic Health Counselor, Yin Yoga teacher, and Kinetic Bridging Specialist.

It's Joanna's mix of American/European sensibilities and knowledge of Eastern/Western medical philosophies that allow her to create customized approaches for her clients, including beautiful recipes. The result is improved health and wellbeing in an incredibly supportive process. Additionally, Joanna makes her own herbal supplements and salves drawing on her knowledge of Ayurvedic treatments and traditional herbalism.

Acknowledgements

In love and gratitude, thank you…

The Nature… for your constant wisdom and guidance.

Alessandro Quargnali-Linsley… my husband and rock, for taking such beautiful pictures of my food, for always saying YES when I bring my ideas to you, and for loving me best.

Daniella Quargnali-Linsley… my daughter, who shows me every day the potential that is available to us all, and who loves to eat (and critique) anything I cook or bake.

Rob and Tom McGovern… my brothers, who have always been my guides, my protectors, and my mirrors, and have never let me forget how special I am to them.

Nancy McGovern… my mama, for knowing just when I need M&Ms or a silly gift, and for finding ways to surround me in magic when I need it most.

Doug McGovern… my dad, for teaching me that I can do anything if I have the right tools, where I can buy or how I can make those tools, and that a cookie is a requirement for all projects.

Teri McGovern… my stepmother, who helps me find the laughter in any situation and believes that all children (and aren't we all someone's child?) should have ice cream whenever they want it.

Martina Faulkner… for encouraging me to share what I do, and helping me share it in such a beautiful way.

Lexi Wurpts… who has spent endless hours keeping me company in my kitchen and garden as I make food, tea, and medicines, for testing so many recipes, and for our deep friendship.

Scott Horwitz… my Twinsicle, my brother from another lifetime, who has walked a parallel path to mine and always been the one to see me, hear me, and love me.

Addie Weaver… who took a chance, and in doing so changed us both as we healed old trauma.

Natalie Furka Padgett… for being the sparkle that never quits sparkling–my eternal glitter, even when sparkle seems impossible for either of us.

Katie Rose… because some friends and friendships defy description, and you are everything.

Patricia Layton… my teacher until her last breath and beyond, who shared my love of flowers and cake, and who shared her light in profound ways.

My friends… who have cooked for me, let me cook for them, and shared many moments over meals.

To all my teachers—past, present, and future—in the traditions I have been welcomed into, and those I have not.

And You… the reader, who has picked up this book, and allowed me to share family meals with you.

Conversion Charts

This is a cookbook about taste, not precision, so all measurements are guidelines. Thus errors in conversion can be addressed by the cook. As an example, most herbs are about 7 grams to the tablespoon, but some are heavier and some are lighter. How it tastes will be your guide on how much to use in future preparations.

When I write down recipes, I tend to do it by Metric weight (especially in baking), because these measurements are more precise than by volume. Americans, however, are taught to cook by volume, and so in an effort to encourage as many people to cook as possible, I listed my recipes here in the Standard system.

Temperature

Standard (American) Temp ^{0}F	Metric Temp ^{0}C
250^0	120^0
320^0	160^0
350^0	180^0
400^0	205^0
425^0	220^0

Measurements

Ingredient	Standard (American)	Metric
MOST spices	1 tablespoon	7 grams
Ginger	1 tablespoon	6 grams
Flour	1 cup	120 grams
Almond Flour	1 cup	90 grams
Baking Soda	½ teaspoon	3 grams
Baking Powder	1 teaspoon	4 grams
Butter	½ cup	115 grams
Chocolate Chips	1 cup	170 grams
Water	1 cup	227 grams
Olive Oil	1 cup	130 grams
OTHERS	1 cup	200 grams

Weight

Standard (American) Weight	Metric Weight
1 ounce	28 grams
1 pound	454 grams
1 teaspoon	5 ml

CPSIA information can be obtained
at www.ICGtesting.com
Printed in the USA
LVHW072034131220
674080LV00021B/212